Souls Reunited

A STORY OF REBIRTH AND REUNION OF SOULS

by
Sue Wakefield

authorHOUSE®

AuthorHouse™ UK Ltd.
500 Avebury Boulevard
Central Milton Keynes, MK9 2BE
www.authorhouse.co.uk
Phone: 08001974150

First published by AuthorHouse 6/4/2007

ISBN: 978-1-4343-0044-7 (sc)

Printed in the United States of America
Bloomington, Indiana

This book is printed on acid-free paper.

Thanks

Special thanks go to Terry Dean whose natural talent for communication made the initial contact possible. I am sure he will make a great medium one day when the constraints of work and a growing family have eased. His sense of humour and patience throughout are an example to us all and I am indebted to him.

My heartfelt thanks also go to Tracey Brooks who made the second part of this story possible. Without her natural gift of clairvoyance, I would not have been able to put "meat on the bones" and retrace my roots, therefore bringing the whole story to life. I am sure that Tracey's encouragement and belief that it would make a brilliant story inspired me throughout.

Last but by no means least, my sincere thanks and love go to my husband, Eddie, for his support throughout and especially on occasions when the computer decided to have a mind of its own due to my basic IT skills!

Author's Note

Some of my words and phrasing may seem rather odd and stilted at times. This is because I wanted to use Wulfgand's words, as and when appropriate. I decided not to use inverted commas when quoting directly from the automatic writing as I felt this would interfere with the flow of the words as they were received.

Introduction

This is a story about a past life as communicated to me by my spirit guide and is set in a period of history that is referred to as the Dark Ages and involves a partnership which spans the centuries of time. Little is known about life in the eighth century in England although the centuries either side seem to be quite well documented. It appears to be a relatively peaceful period in a history of tumultuous times. I hope, that by telling this story, a little light will be shed on these years and on the areas in which it is set as experienced by a few family groups who lived during this time.

It is a story about Wulfgand, a Saxon warrior/farmer who was born in Germany in the eighth century and who eventually settled in a small Cornish village and Griselda whom he met there, fell in love with and married. Griselda's spirit stayed in the land where they lived after she died and was recalled several centuries later by a gentleman practising white witchcraft on the same land. This gentleman brought forward the spirits of the earth and so he was brought together with the spirit of Griselda.

My spirit guide today is Wulfgand and I was his wife Griselda in our former life. The gentleman carrying out the pagan practices was Eddie, my husband in this life.

This is a story of rebirth, reunion and an intertwining of souls right up to the present day.

Part 1

1.

It all began in November 1993 in the Local Government office where I had worked for nearly twenty years and with Terry as my right hand man for fifteen of those years. We had recently moved into the new office block which was built in the grounds of our old offices in the former Guildhall, a rambling red brick building with impressive staircases, an amazing vaulted cellar where the Christmas parties used to take place and attic rooms where at least one departed spirit was seen on a regular basis. The building oozed character and there was purported to be an underground passage from the garden of the Guildhall to the church opposite. A statue marked the spot where the access to the tunnel used to be. The modern new offices and associated car park were actually built on what was the orchard when I originally started work there in 1972. Our office was on the ground floor adjacent to the car park and just about where the orchard would have begun. There were seven of us who worked in this room with our drawing board, registers, files, computers and sundry office paraphernalia around us. We were a happy team and had a good working relationship especially so with Terry and myself. We helped each other through bad times in our separate personal lives and rejoiced in each other's good fortune such as the start of a family and then the birth of other babies as the families grew. Over the years, we became very close, almost like a family ourselves and Terry and I continued to work together side by side through thick and thin. Our spacious new office complete with new furnishings and central heating was a far cry from our cramped conditions in the temporary portacabin or "hut on the lawn" as it was affectionately called, situated on the site of a former tennis court in the garden of the Guildhall.

However, there was something very strange about our brand new office. For months after we moved in, all of us, on a daily basis, were aware of a musty, smoky smell at various times throughout the day. It would appear to be only in one spot at a time and we were actually able to physically walk through the smell! What made this rather odd was the fact that there was a non-smoking policy in all the offices and anyway, it was more of an earthy, smoky smell than that from cigarettes.

This continued and became so bad that we constantly complained to management who eventually asked an engineer to check all the central heating ducts and anything else that could possibly be causing the phenomena. All to no avail. Terry and I have always been interested in spiritual matters and so wondered if there was a spiritual explanation as there certainly was no physical one! I decided, therefore, to invite Ron, a friend of mine, who was a great healer and medium into the office to see if he could sense anything. He certainly did and explained that something happened a long time ago in the orchard (on which our office was standing) and that the spirits were still hanging around and trying to attract our attention. Ron, who was experienced in rescue work, released them and sent them to the light and then looked across the room and saw a monk standing by Terry. Ron then told Terry that he could do this rescue work as well, probably in the form of writing. So, that evening,

Terry sat down with pen and paper and waited expectantly and although he felt something was trying to communicate, no writing was forthcoming.

However, during our lunch hour the following day, I sat with him and almost immediately, he started writing. The message was for me and this was the beginning of an amazing partnership. For four months, sometimes during our lunch break, sometimes after work hours and sometimes even during quiet moments in the day, we held a three-way conversation with a person in the spirit world who became a very dear friend. We always looked forward to our next communication and knew when he was around and waiting for us to choose our time to make contact.

2.

The spirit person who was communicating by automatic writing was using Terry's brain and his body in order to do so. It was especially difficult for him as he spoke in a different tongue and the difficulty was borne out by the erratic size of the writing during the initial communication. Although most of it was legible, it obviously required great effort and took much concentration and energy and left him feeling very tired. After the first few sessions, Terry's arms, legs and feet also felt extremely heavy and tired but gradually returned to normal after about half an hour.

During the first communication, our friend told us that he was from St. Ives in Cornwall and was a relation of mine from long ago in the eighth century. His equivalent name in our language was William and he was a male knight who served the king. William said he was related to me over centuries of history through my family of Yeoman. Now, I knew for a fact and as a result of many years of genealogical research of my family that my ancestors did indeed come from the west country and I have evidence linking them to South Devon in the seventeenth century where they stayed until the late nineteenth century when my great grandparents decided to move to Middlesex. I was now being told that these ancestors of mine were descendants of William from Cornwall. This revelation was mind blowing and I was anxious to learn more but it was obvious that the energy was draining and William was very tired. So we thanked him for talking to us and said goodbye, hoping against hope that he would come through to us again one day. William ended the session by telling Terry that they were a similar type of person. In fact, all through the writing, Terry had a feeling of well being and that William was quite a jolly character. This being the case, they certainly were alike as Terry was renowned for his sense of humour and fun and you could always rely on him to brighten up the day!

We did not have long to wait as the second communication came the next day following a cold shivery sensation down Terry's right side. This was to become a sign that William was ready to come through. This time, William drew a self-portrait of how he looked when he was twenty-eight. It was a sideways view of his face and showed that he had longish hair and a full beard and moustache. We were told that his name was Wulfgand in his tongue and when on earth, he had a wife called Griselda and they had five daughters. William said that he had been searching for years for a family member who reminds him of his beloved Griselda and he has contacted me because I look almost identical. Apparently, he tried to make contact on several occasions during the last twenty years but with no success as conditions were not conducive. Terry now provided that special link and acted as a mediator between us. However, conditions were not ideal as we were often interrupted by work colleagues coming into the office in the middle of a session which resulted in us asking Wulfgand if he could wait! On one occasion, he replied that he would wait for ever but as time went on, it was obvious that the interruptions were detrimental to our communication. We managed as best we could because, after all, how could we explain to our fellow office workers, let alone our managers, that we were talking to a friend who lived in the eighth century!

*Self portrait of Wulfgand and a sample
of the early automatic writing*

The first time that Wulfgand tried to contact me was well over twenty years ago in about 1968 when I was living with girls of my age. It made me feel heady – not right - with bad heads, he said. A little figure was drawn of me in a long dress with longish hair and underneath was written "flower power" with several sketches of flowers! This amused me as I was going through my hippy stage and the flower power era of the late 60's. Moreover, I did live with friends of a similar age as four of us shared a flat in a large Victorian house.

Wulfgand said that the bond between us was very strong and he was almost certain that I was his wife before. The reason that I have no children in this life, he said, is because I died giving birth to our fifth child in our past life together in Cornwall. By this time, the hairs on the back of my neck started to stand on end as I realised the implications of what was being written. For many years, I have been fascinated by the idea of reincarnation and would like to have been regressed by hypnosis if I could have found someone trustworthy enough but somehow, it just never happened. Now, a past life was being unfolded before me in a way that I never dreamt of. The karmic reason for not being blessed with children intrigued me and indeed explained a lot. From an early age, I have enjoyed being with and working with children and always wanted the idyllic image of a large family of my own. However, I used to say to friends and family that I was not keen on babies and giving birth but would like children "ready made" from the age of about two years. Although there was no medical reason as to why I should not conceive, the fact is that I never did which in itself, caused great heartache. I used to tell myself that it was for a very good reason that I was not meant to have a family of my own. I decided to let nature take care of things and if it was not meant to be then it just was not meant to be! It was now obvious to me that a past life memory was lingering in my psyche – that of my own traumatic death during childbirth. No wonder I did not want to chance going through it again in this life! With the benefit of this knowledge, it would appear that I had a very good reason not to conceive and I found this strangely comforting. As anyone in a similar situation would do, I found myself questioning on numerous occasions the reason why I could not have a family. Now at last, I knew why and it was as if a light was illuminating my life and all was becoming clear. In an odd way, I felt I had come full circle.

3.

As Wulfgand became more used to Terry, communication was easier and the writing became neater and easier to read. Wulfgand liked to test Terry's artistic ability by drawing several sketches and although simplistic, they conveyed the idea and meaning very well. For instance, I asked what his armour was like and he immediately sketched a figure complete with helmet and with his main weapons by his side which were a spear, a sword, an axe and a shield. He even drew his horse's head and neck! Wulfgand told Terry that he did very well for a beginner and with practise he would become much better!

Wulfgand's armour and weapons

Throughout the writings so far, two symbols appeared on a regular basis and usually at the beginning of a sentence or while we were asking a question. One of these symbols was a multi pointed star and the other looked like an axe. The significance of these symbols intrigued me especially when I was told that the axe like object was a symbol of our life together. All marriages have this – a blessing and I would remember this if I went back. I still did not really understand except that the axe was an important tool and weapon in those days as was shown by the previous drawing of his armour and weapons. The multi pointed star remained a mystery even though I was told that I would recognise it and that if I found the old village site, there may be a reminder left.

Wulfgand was born in the north eastern part of Germany which we know as Saxony. The area, similar to our counties was called Bundalinia, a name that I have not, as yet, had any luck in tracing. Many of them travelled overseas like an army and settled in Cornwall where I was already living as a Celt. Apparently, the chief of the village married us when I was fifteen years old and we had a happy, albeit short, life together. Most of my time was spent looking after the children but I loved flowers and was always picking them. I can relate to this as I love flowers and gardening and being close to nature. Several years ago, I had a hobby of collecting flowers, pressing them and using them to decorate bookmarks, pictures, paper weights etc. I found it extremely therapeutic just as I do today when I am gardening and amongst flowers. So it seems that my love of flowers has carried over into my present incarnation.

Inbetween fighting in minor battles and skirmishes, Wulfgand worked on the smallholding and went out hunting for food. The village at St. Ives where we lived was much smaller than today and consisted of about twenty people, some of whom were neutral Celts. Wulfgand sketched a layout of the village which shows a village sign beside a path leading across to the main entrance to the village site which was circular in shape enclosed by a fence on the perimeter. Inside the main entrance on the left was an animal pen and the houses are round in shape and situated on the outskirts of the site. In the centre is a building that was used as a meeting hall. An enlarged version of the emblem at the village entrance was drawn in some detail. Our house was like a wooden stick hut and we kept chickens and pigs. We ate well by all accounts and sometimes had venison.

The picture of our village life was beginning to build up and all the information we received so far was fascinating. As neither Terry or myself knew anything about the life and times of the eighth century, I decided it was time to do some research to see if I could corroborate what we had been told. However, it was another eight months before my research began. In hindsight, the delay was obviously engineered by a higher force as the final drawing from the spirit world was, in my opinion, important evidence of a genuine communication.

4.

During the initial communication, Wulfgand told us that he was a male knight and served the king. In a later session when asked how he became a knight, he added that first he worked on the farm then showed courage in a small fight against the Celts near the border of Devon and was then honoured by the king of the area. A coat of arms was drawn which had a cross shape in the middle dividing it into four parts. In each part was a different symbol. This coat of arms originated from Germany and is made up of the four regions of Germanic society. Each section denotes a region and the region that Wulfgand came from was the top right hand section.

Wulfgand said that he died in battle in Wales in 763 AD. The Celts tried to invade England so they attacked them but Cornwall was beaten and the battle was lost to the Celts. Cornish was not spoken as the victor's tongue. It was a great honour to die in battle.

This all sounded totally plausible but as neither Terry or I had a clue about the history of the period, we had no way of knowing, at that time, if any of it bore any resemblance to the era.

I was intrigued as to know what the spirit world was like and if Wulfgand did any work there and if so, what sort of work. When I asked him what it is like where he is, he replied that it is beautiful and full of peace and that I must not worry about going to join him. When asked about his work, Wulfgand told us that he was an overseer at the entrance to the light and had been doing this work for many moons. His work consisted of checking the spirits entering from the earth plane so that no bad spirits went in. Because of the type of work that he did, he could come and go as he pleased and so was able to talk to us frequently. I asked why he had not progressed further in spirit and was told that it was because he was looking for me. Now that he had found me, he was much happier but wanted to stay a little longer because he just liked being close.

I was fascinated by what life could be like in the spirit world and wanted to learn more. As Terry and I sat down in January 1994 for the first session after Christmas, Wulfgand took quite a long time coming through which was unusual. Apparently, he was far away, seeing people over. I asked how he knew when we were trying to contact him and he said it was like air waves or thought vibrations. Wulfgand was aware that we had just celebrated Christmas but told us that he was not really a Christian but a non believer of any when on earth and that he feels the same now. No one has control, it just happens. Wulfgand then went on to say that they are not allowed to give too much away as everybody has to find out for himself.

On the subject of why I came back to earth, Wulfgand said that we all come back to learn and this is my time to learn. Everyone has something of their own to learn even though we all feel as if it is a waste of time and wonder why we are here. No one sends us back to earth, it just happens when necessary. Wulfgand could see our future but would not tell us about it as this would be a bad omen. We have to wait and see then if it is not right, we have to try again.

5.

Wulfgand sounded very caring in his communications and gave us advice on several occasions. Just before Christmas 1993, I developed mysterious red patches all over my body and I could think of nothing that might have caused it. When I mentioned it to Wulfgand, he said it was an allergy and that it would go shortly by working its way out of my body. This proved correct and thankfully, the unsightly patches gradually disappeared soon after.

During a session later that month, I told Wulfgand that I was having trouble sleeping and he immediately wrote that my mind was restless and that I need to relax more and take time out for myself. During this particular time, I liked to send out healing thoughts to those in need just before going to sleep but I was advised to leave it for a while until I was sleeping better. The efficacy depends on strength of thought and when tired, the strength is low. Wulfgand said that I was a good listener and helped people cope in general.

At the beginning of February 1994, we asked advice on behalf of a work colleague who was having problems of a psychic nature at her home. The problems seemed to be linked to her teenage daughter who was given a crystal while on holiday abroad and told it came from a religious site. However, the crystal had mysteriously disappeared.

Wulfgand said he had been told about the situation and that the crystal was no good and it must be disposed of. It was the wrong crystal for her and was not akin. Apparently, the crystal was not lost but hidden and would appear within the next couple of weeks. We had to tell the mother to help and not let her daughter touch it. The mother was then instructed to dispose of the crystal after blessing it but not near her daughter. The advice was to put it in a lake where the force would be diffused and no harm done. We were somewhat alarmed by these instructions and so asked if the crystal was bad. The reply was that it all depends on the use and this particular crystal was not used correctly and given after evil worship. This story does have a satisfactory ending as the crystal did reappear in a drawer within a couple of weeks and the mother followed Wulfgand's instructions and threw it in a large lake after blessing it. After this event, negative activity in the house seemed to decrease and finally cleared altogether.

As the weeks went by, the writing was flowing freely and Wulfgand sometimes came through very quickly. This was when the passage was clear and he praised Terry and said he was doing well. On occasions, Wulfgand came too early, before we were ready and this was when Terry felt very heavy and knew that Wulfgand was waiting. Sometimes, Wulfgand was a long time coming through and on odd occasions, did not come through at all. This was because he was seeing people over. There were many others doing this work and they communicate with each other by thought transference which is much faster than the spoken word.

Several years earlier, I went to see a psychic artist who drew a beautiful portrait of a guide who was with me at the time. His name was something similar to "Saren" he thought. I decided to take the drawing to our next session to see what Wulfgand had to say about him and even, if he could see the drawing. First of all, the drawing was positioned in front of me out of Terry's sight and Wulfgfand said he could not see it as he was "in Terry and not free". So I placed the drawing in front of Terry and asked if he could see it now. The answer was yes and he continued to say that this is a wise guide who went over to spirit in 1760 aged 84 years. His name was Sarendah Singh and he was a Hindu – a holy priest and lived in Kathmandu. At first, he was like a chief of a village then became a holy man. Sarendah came to help me in 1966 when I, unknowingly, called for help. My life at the time was distressed and not simple – a jumbled mess! I felt quite touched and said I should be very grateful to which Wulfgand replied that he knows. I could relate to the description of my life being a jumbled mess as at that particular time I was going through a long period of mental depression when my self esteem was at an all time low and I felt that life was not worth living. I drifted through a couple of years in a haze as a result of medication and most of the time feeling in despair and suicidal. I was unaware then that Sarendah came to help me through those bad times but I do remember something else from those days. It was one day when I was at my lowest ebb and I was lying on a sofa at my parents' home feeling extremely sorry for myself when I was aware of a face looking down at me. It seemed to be the face of an archetypal cherub and was full of love and peace. With hindsight, this was the point that my mental health started to improve and I gradually resumed a normal life. I am convinced that this spirit or angel or cherub or whatever was sent to give me strength when I most needed it. So perhaps this was the work of my guide, Sarendah who was not my main guide however. We on earth have many helpers round us depending on the situation and as time goes by, they move on and are replaced by others.

My main guide at the time was a nun who died in the early 1800's at an early age. She was English but born of Czechoslovakian parents and was known as "Holkavoc" which was her surname – no one knew her first name! She lived south of London in Surrey (where incidentally I lived until the age of 23 years) and came to me because of likeness of mind about 23 years previously which was around the time of my first marriage. This guide had made contact with me on an earlier occasion I was told and indeed she had as I recalled.

On the subject of spirit communication in general, Wulfgand said that it is only possible if the departed loved one wants to make contact. For example, I asked if he could bring my grandmother forward and he said yes but only if she wanted to come.

One evening while Terry was at home with his wife and family, an amusing incident took place. He was upstairs in the bedroom, the children were asleep and his wife was downstairs when he heard someone calling his name very softly. As he thought it was his wife calling quietly up the stairs so as not to wake the children, to see if he wanted a cup of tea, Terry called out "I'll be down in a minute". However, the voice continued in almost a whisper so Terry eventually went down to find his wife sitting on the sofa and no tea in sight. "Where is it then – the cup of tea? I thought I heard you calling me" he said to his wife who looked totally blank as she had not left the room at all and had not called out to him either. At the session with Wulfgand on the following day, I told him what had happened and he replied that Terry did hear voices but that he could not understand it. It was his guardian, a lady and it would be clearer next time. Wulfgand would not tell us anymore about her but just said that she will tell Terry in time but that it was her who left a supporting message a few days earlier. It would appear that only certain messages and information were allowed to be told to us and that the time had to be right and when we were ready for it.

6.

As the weeks passed, not only were we in regular contact with Wulfgand who we felt was becoming a close friend but other earthbound spirits were communicating through Terry's automatic writing. These spirits had passed over but appeared to be in limbo and were confused about their situation. Terry spoke to them all mentally, blessed them and sent them forward on their journey towards the light. This is the rescue work that Ron initially told Terry that he would be able to do and he dealt with many lost souls over the course of three to four months. We asked Wulfgand if he saw over all the spirits that Terry rescued to which he replied in the negative but others told him about it and they were all being logged. It seemed that Terry's work was being taken notice of.

We were still experiencing the mysterious smell of smoke in the office at odd times during the day but now knew that this was made by the spirits waiting to go over, in order to attract Terry's attention. It would appear that as Terry released them, the news travelled fast to others! Wulfgand was aware of my friend Ron who also helped many lost souls and said that they all smile down on both Ron and Terry for their good work.

I asked if I would ever be able to do any psychic work and was told yes, in the future but not yet. It would be similar to Terry's and it would come naturally as it did to Terry. The time was not right for me and with hindsight, I can understand why. It was an upsetting time for me in my personal life when a rocky marriage seemed to be even rockier and the future was very uncertain. The conditions were obviously not conducive to spirit communication.

Not long after our initial contact, I visited my friend Ron, a healer and clairvoyant. During the evening while we were discussing the automatic writing that was forthcoming, Ron was aware of a spirit presence and he thought it was Wulfgand. At the session on the following day, Wulfgand confirmed that he was at Ron's on the previous evening and that he tried to be visual. He said that he would try again on another occasion and also would try to be visual to Terry in the future. About a month later, Wulfgand was as good as his word and appeared to Terry in a dream along with various objects such as the village sign and symbols as drawn on previous occasions. He showed his face only, complete with long reddish hair and full beard and moustache. Terry reproduced the portrait and accompanying symbols the following day for me to see. Wulfgand wrote that he appeared to Terry as he felt that we needed proof to carry on and that he came late so as not to scare others by which we presume he meant Terry's family and for which we were grateful. It was a timely appearance as we tried to keep level headed throughout and even though we felt the contact was genuine and the character trustworthy, at times it seemed such an amazing experience that I suppose, in truth, there was an element of doubt as to the source. It was a tribute to Wulfgand that he picked up on this which we took to be a sign of our developing friendship.

As the weeks progressed, our regular discussions with our spirit friend seemed as natural as talking to someone in the next office! We both felt totally at ease during the sessions and looked forward to the messages, guidance, information and answers to our many questions that were conveyed through automatic writing. It was becoming a fascinating part of our life which made us feel both humble and privileged to be part of such a wonderful and unique experience. It came as somewhat of a shock, therefore, when the writing suddenly ceased with no warning and Wulfgand no longer came through. The last communication ended with Wulfgand saying that he was tired. We did not realize this was the last communication of course and that same evening I visited Ron to keep him abreast of developments of which he was most interested. Ron said that it was obvious that I had not heard the last of Wulfgand and that he felt a partnership was being cemented. There was a great deal of power there and Ron felt that Wulfgand was keeping in the background but was organising things.

However, no more automatic writing was forthcoming and Terry and I felt quite bereft! We continued to sit at odd times in the hope that Wulfgand would return but to no avail. Two weeks later we were rewarded by an intriguing communication. First of all, a sketch appeared of a head and shoulders which resembled a heavenly being, looking down on another drawing of a face with long hair and full beard wearing a beaver type hat. A line connected this face to the words "Gone – reborn" and the message was signed "friend". From this, we deduced that Terry's guide or friend as she always signed herself, was telling us that Wulfgand had gone away and was reborn. The drawing was obviously Wulfgand but the hat he was wearing was unfamiliar. It looked like a woolly hat with a long pointed bit sticking up on top! Both Terry and I felt very grateful for this confirmation but also felt rather confused and somewhat alarmed by the word "reborn". Did it mean he was being reborn on the earth plane? If so, why did he not tell us? In any case, why did he not tell us that he was going away wherever it was. Once again, that same evening, I informed Ron of the latest news. The last time I was there which was after Wulfgand's final communication, Ron kept something back from me. Apparently, he had the impression that Wulfgand was going to disappear for a while as he was going on a learning course to get greater control. Ron said he desperately wants to do more but was unable – he made a contract and will stick to it.

*This drawing and message marked the
end of the automatic writing*

In the light of this information, it would seem that Wulfgand was not going to reincarnate on earth but was striving to learn how to improve communication. Perhaps this meant that he would have to be reborn onto another level in order to gain knowledge. Whatever it meant, it was obvious that the regular sessions of automatic writing had come to an end and for this, Terry and I felt extremely sad and wondered if we would ever hear from him again. The fact that Wulfgand appeared to Ron as well as communicating through Terry, gave the whole experience more credence and helped to dispel any doubts that we may have had.

At odd times during the following months, Terry and I sat quietly with pencil and paper in the faint hope that Wulfgand would come through but nothing was forthcoming. However, a year later, another picture appeared of a bearded face wearing a helmet complete with nose piece and underneath was written "soon return". The date was 24th November 1994.

7.

The time now seemed right to carry out some research into the period of history in which Wulfgand and Griselda lived. The inner quest to search for the village site at St. Ives in Cornwall was also very strong and although Wulfgand had promised to guide me and to help locate the site on a map by using a pendulum, it was to be eleven years before I travelled down to Cornwall. Instead, I wrote to several organisations in St. Ives inquiring about the existence of a village sign to see if there were any similarities to the eighth century sign! My enquiries did not lead anywhere unfortunately but I was informed of the ancient village site of Chysauster which was situated between Penzance and St. Ives. This Celtic settlement was originally occupied two thousand years ago and consisted of eight stone walled homesteads which form one of the oldest village streets in the country. As interesting as this site is, archaeological evidence reveals that it was occupied up to 400 AD which is much earlier than my previous life in Cornwall. Although it was exciting to find the site of an ancient village in the vicinity of St. Ives, I did not feel particularly drawn to it but nevertheless, kept all informative leaflets for future reference.

I now turned my attention to the age of the eighth century which was part of the Anglo Saxon period in England. As Wulfgand had already revealed that he was born in Germany and pinpointed an area to the north-east, I presumed that he came from Saxony. The Saxons were a group of pagan warrior-farmers who came across the North Sea originally at the invitation of the Romans who needed them to help protect their crumbling empire from other raiders. Angles and Saxons arrived over a long period of time – some to conquer and fight for a settlement, others to occupy lands secured by their kinsfolk. They came in independent bands each under its own leader. They established independent kingdoms under its own king or prince. Early accounts of Germanic society describe chiefs attended by retinues of wellborn young men who formed their war bands. Having left their kindred, the protection of the lord and companionship of others created new bonds of loyalty. The lord was expected to reward his followers generously and loyalty was the highest virtue. These ideas were brought over to Britain with migration.

The pagan Germans believed that their kings were descended from gods and had supernatural force and so any male member of a royal family was eligible for kingship. These beliefs were still held in eighth century Britain.

From 500AD onwards, the Celtic inhabitants of Britain were driven into Cornwall, Wales, Strathclyde and Scotland by Anglo Saxon newcomers who settled in the east and south in what was later called England. Some Britons were enslaved, some fled overseas, some to forests, some to offshore islands but most to "the high hills, steep and fortified", the old Iron Age hillforts which were abandoned when the Romans first conquered Britain.

By the time Wulfgand arrived in Cornwall sometime in the first half of the eighth century, most of southern Britain except Devon, Cornwall and Wales was under Anglo Saxon control. Names in Cornwall and Wales are overwhelmingly

Celtic as these were the last areas to be dominated by the English and the native population (i.e. the Celts) was much larger here than other areas as the pace of conquest diminished. In Dumnonia, the Cornish peninsular, a separate Celtic kingdom emerged whose people lived in "rounds" which were a type of defended farmstead-cum-homestead similar to the "raths" of Ireland.

There was a parallel between the Celts and the Saxons as they were both part of the same European rootstock. They both had lifestyles coloured by the presence of Rome over a couple of centuries but returned to their own level of society. At the lowest peasant levels, the subsistence farmers would have had everything in common. There would be small difference to the landsman whether the lord of the manor was a Roman tax collector, a Celtic war lord or a Saxon chieftain.

Wulfgand came across the North Sea with a group of others to settle in Cornwall which at first I found perplexing as Cornwall at that time was a separate kingdom keeping its Celtic roots. However, bearing in mind the basic similarity between the two races and evidence of intermarriage between Anglo Saxons and Britons (Celts), it would appear that it was possible for the native and the newcomer to co-exist peacefully. In his writings, Wulfgand said that some Celts in his village were neutral which seems to bear this out.

Although many battles were fought between the Saxons and the Britons during the eighth century, it was not until 838AD at the Battle of Hingston Down that Egbert, king of Wessex, defeated the Britons of Cornwall and the last episode in the story of the English conquest of Britain was accomplished. Wulfgand was purported to have died in battle against the Celts in Wales in 763AD. This appears quite feasible as there were many battles and skirmishes on the borders of Wales at this time and as a result, the famous Offa's Dyke was built to keep the Welsh out. By all accounts, the year of 763AD was the year of a severe winter when travel ceased for four months as snow and ice lay in a thick carpet all over Europe. Food ran out and people died of starvation. Even if Wulfgand had survived the battle, the hardship of the winter weather that same year would have been extremely difficult to endure.

8.

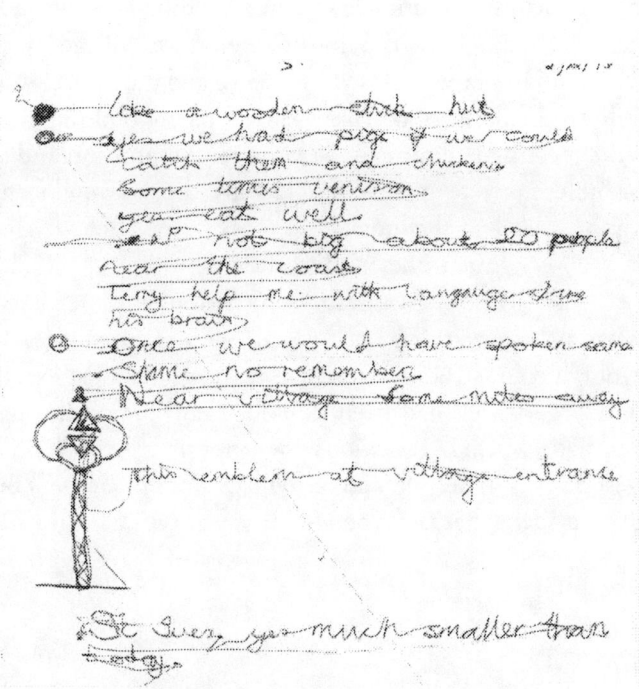

Village sign and automatic writing

Not too far away from where I live is a reconstructed Anglo Saxon village at West Stow which I thought would be worth a visit to give some insight into the daily life of the times. On entering the village site at the end of a long path at the beginning of which was a village sign carved out of rock, I was struck by the similarity of the approach compared to Wulfgand's sketch of our village in Cornwall. Our village also had a sign positioned at the start of a long approach road which ended at the main gate. I was even more amazed as I walked through the main entrance to the village site and noticed that immediately to the left was an animal enclosure positioned exactly according to Wulfgand's sketch. The similarity did not stop here as the village layout was round in shape enclosed by a fence and the houses were built on the perimeter. There was a separate building used as the meeting hall more or less in a central position and all the buildings were made of timber with strips of wood forming the walls and the long, steep roofs were thatched. They looked very much like Wulfgand's description of wooden stick huts. By now, I was wandering around in somewhat of a daze as I realized that I was in an Anglo Saxon village, the layout and construction of which resembled almost exactly the village which had been described and drawn through automatic writing. It obviously was not the same village, as West Stow is in Suffolk and our village was in Cornwall but it was evident that the type of village was typical of the era.

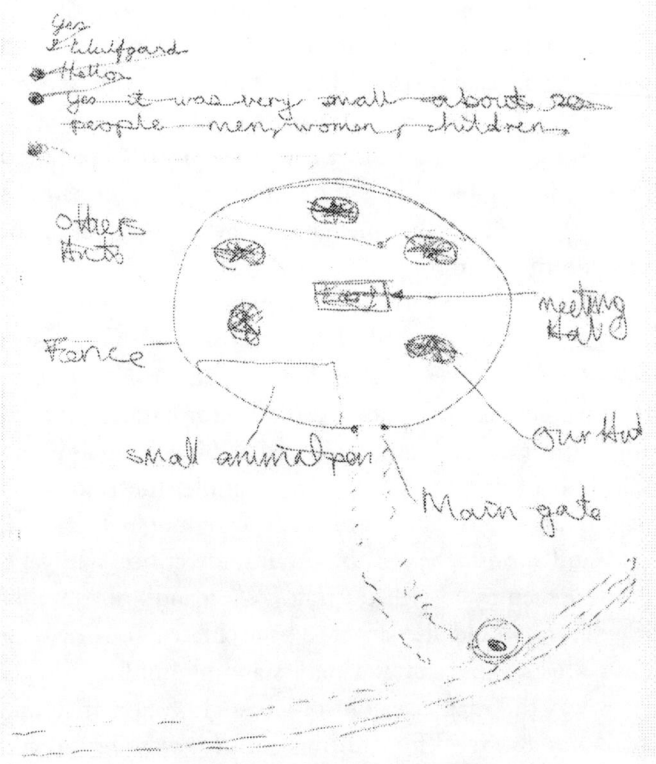

Village layout and automatic writing

The written information of everyday life that I picked up at West Stow was enlightening but more of that in a while. The most outstanding moment of the whole visit was when I picked up a postcard in the shop which portrayed a man in Saxon clothes sitting outside one of the houses crafting objects from wood and antlers with a knife. What caught my attention immediately was the strange type of woollen hat with pointed end that he was wearing. It was exactly the headgear that was portrayed by Terry's spirit friend when she told us that Wulfgand had gone and was to be reborn.

This was really the climax of the visit as it was corroboration of detail given to us by spirit. As I pointed out earlier, my knowledge of Anglo Saxon life and times was non existent, as was Terry's, so we were somewhat nonplussed when faced with a sketch showing headgear which looked suspiciously like a modern bobble hat without the bobble! This particular piece of evidence gave me renewed belief and trust in our spirit communication.

There was more corroboration of facts to come as I read through the literature that I had collected at West Stow. Although there is very little evidence to tell us about daily life in Anglo Saxon England, certain information has been deduced from grave goods and similar finds which give an indication of some aspects. For example, the traditional image of an Anglo Saxon is of a man with long hair and full beard and moustache. This certainly describes Wulfgand as can be seen by his self-portrait. Wulfgand's portrayal of his weapons would also deem to be accurate as one of West Stow's illustrations shows a man standing holding a spear which was the main weapon of all Anglo Saxon men and which was also used for hunting. Shields were round and made from wood sometimes with a leather covering. Other weapons necessary to everyday life were a sword and an axe. The axe was a very important and symbolic tool which was mentioned by Wulfgand on more than one occasion.

The Anglo Saxons lived in a rural society with an economy based on agricultural production. Most people's lives were dominated by farming, looking after animals and growing crops with variations in routine according to the season. Everyone was involved in farming and most craft objects were produced for domestic use and perhaps some for trade. This subsistence lifestyle would have been very hard. This would concur with Wulfgand's description of working on the smallholding which included having pigs and chickens.

Hunting was a major part of an Anglo Saxon man's life and Wulfgand admitted to sometimes having venison and in general, his family ate well.

Height is a good indicator of nutrition and a poor diet will result in people not growing to their maximum potential. It is often assumed that people in the past were much smaller than they are today. Skeletal evidence can tell us how tall the Anglo Saxons were and it shows that the average man and woman living in the 690's is about the same height as today's average man and woman.

Anglo Saxon families were often large with many children. Wealthy men and women could show off their fine clothes, jewellery and weapons but most families had to make do with simpler things. Life expectancy was a lot shorter than it is today. The average age of death for an Anglo Saxon man was thirty-five while women had a shorter life expectancy of thirty. Pregnancy and childbirth could be hazardous and life threatening. Evidence suggests that one third of children died by the age of six and fifty per cent of men and women died between the ages of nineteen and thirty- five. However, some people lived to a ripe old age of about sixty.

The high mortality rates reflect the susceptibility of the Anglo Saxon population to a wide range of diseases and ailments. Wounds and burns must have been hazards as well as coughs and bronchial problems which would have been exacerbated by woodsmoke in the dark, ill ventilated houses. The harsh environment and hard physical work resulted in the early onset of osteoarthritis and there was a constant risk of food shortage and malnutrition. It is possible that people suffered from vitamin deficiencies in winter and early spring because of their diet at that time of year. It seems that I was a victim of the dangers of childbirth as I died giving birth to our fifth child in the mid 700's. With the absence of modern medicine and knowledge, it must have been a harrowing experience for many poor women. No wonder not many reached the age of thirty. The men were also threatened everytime they left their smallholdings to join in a battle or minor skirmish as the warrior farmers were obliged to do. Wounds and battle scars were commonplace and these were often life threatening without the benefit of modern technology to treat them. The chance of being killed outright in battle was, of course, very high as my former husband Wulfgand knows, to his cost. It appears that both our lives ended in a very typical manner of the period.

There were many unasked questions about my past life and family for which I longed to have answers. What happened to my children when I died? Did I have parents, brothers, sisters? I wanted to know more about my husband, how we met and about his family. However, this was a lesson in patience for me and of believing that all would be revealed when the time was right. I am not the most patient of people at times so this was quite a steep learning curve! I was told that Wulfgand had gone away but would return a lot stronger and this I believed although it was another eight years and after major changes in my personal life that we became reacquainted.

Part II

1.

As the automatic writing came to an end, so life itself became increasingly complicated and hectic. Office life was busier as the work load became more complex and responsibility grew with the work load. There were now no spare moments in the day and our lunch breaks were short so that spirit communication was out of the question even if there was anyone around to communicate! By this time, my twenty five year old marriage was in tatters and divorce proceedings were in place. I now had to take on a large mortgage in order to stay in the marital home as my elderly parents were living next door in a self contained annexe and I was trying to protect them from any upheaval related to the divorce. My job now became more important to me as my personal responsibilities increased and I tried to focus on it as much as possible. The support of my friends at this time was a tower of strength and one friend in particular grew closer and closer as we realised how much we had in common both spiritually and in the physical world which included both our motorbikes! Three years later, this friend became my husband and another major event took place as we decided to sell my property and move into his converted barns. Much heart seeking went on over this decision as it meant moving my parents who were now eighty two years of age. I was fortunate in finding the ideal bungalow for them just three miles from where I was to live. It was a relief to me that they loved their new home and continued to enjoy it for many more years. I am a strong believer that events take place in life when the time is right and although this move seemed daunting and unsettling for my parents at the time, I realize, with hindsight, that it was the best thing that could have happened as shortly afterwards my mother had a stroke and would definitely not have been able to cope with stairs anymore.

My new life with my new family, which included three adult stepchildren and many relations on my husband's side, was so different to the one I had been used to and I felt extremely fortunate to be in such a position. I now had the large family and "children" that I had always wanted and our financial position was such that we were able to travel widely and realize personal dreams such as visiting Nepal and India and seeing the mighty Himalayas for ourselves. India held a special place in my heart as my mother and grandparents lived there for many years in the early twentieth century and so it was a sentimental journey that took us to Darjeeling to follow in their footsteps.

Over a period of time, we decided to make alterations and extend the house to make provision for a growing family as grandchildren were now appearing on a regular basis! Life continued to be very rushed as we both had full time jobs, a house and half an acre of garden to tend as well as keeping a close eye on my parents and helping them out as much as possible. Many weekends were spent visiting various family members in different parts of the country and there never seemed to be enough hours in the day. So when an opportunity to take early retirement presented itself, we grabbed it with both hands and said goodbye to our working life in local government for over thirty years and settled in to a more relaxed lifestyle. I now had the spare time in which to pursue my spiritual interests during which I made new friends and learned much.

A few months before I retired, a work colleague whose father had recently died, told me of a brilliant medium and clairvoyant whom she had visited and received outstanding evidence from spirit. As this medium lived but a few miles from me, I decided to book an appointment to see what general information I might receive. I was suitably impressed by my first visit and felt a rapport with Tracey from the beginning. Nine months later, I booked another reading and this was to be a turning point in my life and the start of many visits to Tracey which increased in regularity.

2.

My second visit to Tracey took place on 21ˢᵗ November 2002. I looked forward to the reading and wondered who would come through and what the Tarot cards had to say this time. Before each visit, I made a point of relaxing and going with a completely open mind. As soon as we settled down, Tracey said she had someone from spirit who had a connection with a gentleman in an office who did automatic writing and that we were linked but going back a long way. The spirit person was showing pages of writing but Tracey could not read it as it was an unidentifiable language and looked like old calligraphy of some sort. Tracey told me that I was gifted and had spiritual work to do and she could sense healing and crystals all around me. By now, I felt quite excited as I was sure the spirit must be Wulfgand and the gentleman in an office who did automatic writing must be Terry. I was hoping for more evidence but Tracey went on to other spirits who were waiting to come through and so I had to be patient. I was told that my journey had just begun and that some sort of travelling would be involved which would be a spiritual lesson for me. At the end of the card reading, Tracey asked if I had any questions. I asked if she could contact someone if I said a name to which she replied that she would try, so I said "Wulfgand". The immediate response was a description of a man in a beaver type hat with a tail who speaks in a different tongue – something like Gaelic or Celtic. His voice was deep and he had a moustache and carried a wooden axe or a club. Tracey then became very excited and cried "That's it – it wasn't calligraphy – it was this language – a different dialect!" Wulfgand was wearing a sort of overall tunic and had criss crossed straps on his legs. This was exactly as he portrayed himself nine years earlier when showing us what his armour was like. I asked why he went away before and he replied that he had to leave suddenly and pull back from the man but will show himself again. Wulfgand then disappeared into Tracey's kitchen! Tracey then recalled that two to three weeks earlier which was about the time that I phoned to book an appointment, she had a dream which she thought strange as it was set such a long time ago. In the dream, Tracey was outside a stick hut in a village which was situated near water and she was standing with a woman who was slim and had long hair and who was wearing a long brown gown and some sort of tooth necklace. Tracey's description of a stick hut in a village was identical to Wulfgand's description of his house through his earlier automatic writing. Tracey thought that the dream was very significant and that Wulfgand was preparing her for my visit.

I was thrilled that Wulfgand had made contact again – almost exactly nine years after the initial communication. The last message from Terry's spirit friend that said Wulfgand would return and also Ron's prediction that he was going away for a while in order to be stronger both proved to be correct and this was my first lesson in learning to put my trust in spirit.

3.

It was another sixteen months before I saw Tracey again by which time I was enjoying my early retirement and had joined a weekly meditation class which gradually introduced me to many aspects of spiritual work and interest. My fascination with crystals began at about this time and I read as much as possible as well as attending a crystal workshop which was very informative and where we had a chance to be shown practical application. My crystal collection grew and grew and I found them very beautiful and therapeutic and used them in everyday life. Sixteen months earlier, Tracey saw crystals around me but at the time I had little interest and no knowledge about them. However, doors were opened and my interests expanded so maybe this was another lesson in trusting spirit!

On the morning of my next visit to Tracey, she phoned early to say that there had been a cancellation and would I like to go an hour earlier to which I agreed. As soon as we sat down, a gentleman came through from the higher planes who Tracey said was a guide. He had blond hair and a beard and lived in a round house. He lived a long way back in Saxon times and did not understand Tracey as he spoke a different language. This person had communicated before but went back at one point but has come forward now to start being close again. He said that I have more time now and I am ready to work. Tracey said there has been a connection before and that our past lives were linked but now he is on a spiritual working level. There was a definite link with a past life as Tracey could see me standing outside a hut with a long low roof and no windows and said that it was an encampment by the sea. Tracey felt that the gentleman (or Wulfgand as this must be him) had a strong nature and was known by strength of character. He had quite a bubbly personality and a nice feeling about him but said that I have not been aware of him. When I asked what signs would he give me, he replied that lights would go up and down and he liked to be close to my hair. Tracey said that Wulfgand feels happy to make contact today but is saying that not all is made clear as yet and that my spiritual journey is just beginning. Tracey felt that Wulfgand was very strong and spiritually gifted and is working with me and recommended that I do a self awareness course as I am ready to work. She felt that inspirational writing was for me and also felt that I would be quite good at trance therefore meditation is good. We continued to have a very enlightening session when I was given much general guidance and told that I do have a gift but do not like a lot of people around me. Tracey said that she could see me writing and that I am unique and will understand when I start to work. How right she was but another seventeen months went by before her words came true.

At this point, I would like to make clear that Tracey gives hundreds of readings in a year and very rarely remembers individuals unless of course they are regulars nor does she remember what is said during a reading. So when she started to describe Wulfgand this time, she had no recollection of who he was until I enlightened her at the close of the reading. As my visits became more frequent with Wulfgand communicating each time, Tracey came to recognise him straightaway.

Towards the end of this session, Tracey asked if I had any links with Cornwall at which I laughed and said it was Wulfgand again. The cancelled appointment that morning happened for the very good reason that the first appointment of the day would provide the higher energy needed for my guide to come through.

I left this session feeling very privileged and looked forward to a positive and hopeful future as I trod my spiritual path.

4.

With hindsight, Wulfgand reappeared in my present life about the time that the subject of early retirement from work was broached. It was as if he knew that I would shortly be free of work restraints and have the time to pursue my personal interests. I am sure he was preparing me for our future work together. This reinforced my belief that events happen, mostly, when the time and conditions are right and not before. With no work worries and a more relaxed lifestyle, my mind was clear and concentration easier.

Five months later in August 2004, I felt an urge to have another reading with Tracey to see if Wulfgand would come through again to tell me more. So I booked an appointment and again, as soon as we sat down, Tracey was whisked to a higher plane and was working with guides. A gentleman came forward with long, reddish fair hair and a beard and he lived in Saxon times. He showed a round house with a fire in the middle which was located in Cornwall. Tracey could hear him saying "Nor" but he did not speak our language so telepathic interpretation was quite difficult. It seemed that Wulfgand was indeed here again.

Tracey said that she had a dream a few nights ago about this place that was now being shown to her. In the dream, she could see cliffs, high land, the sea and round houses.

Someone died having a baby and there seemed to be lots of children standing around. This was Wulfgand's way of preparing Tracey for my visit, just as he did once before.

Wulfgand was smiling and said that he had been looking for me and has come back for me but has more to say and wants to feel close. A dark stone was brought forward which looked like a bit of coal – nothing fancy because I do not need it as I already have the gift but must clear my mind. My spiritual gift is wide ranging and involves higher energy but I have to get in tune, I was told. This was relevant as I often had problems with trying to stop the constant chatter of my mind during meditation.

Wulfgand kept saying what sounded like "Nor man" and he showed signs written on flint. Some of the writing was written from top to bottom rather than across and he said that they left signs on stones in another country which showed the way from one country to another. Several of them came over the sea in a long wooden boat, landed and made their home. The words "Nar vik" and "Nor man" were heard. When I asked in what part of Cornwall did he live, Tracey said it was westerly and she could again see high land, cliffs and the sea. Also, she could see a slim lady with long hair and facial features like mine, wearing a long gown fastened with a pin. It was Wulfgand's woman who died having a child and to whom he was dedicated. Tracey said he really loved that woman who resembled me but whose hair was longer. Wulfgand said he is going to work with me as we are very close by virtue of a reincarnation on my part. His character came over as being very strong and a dominating presence.

It seemed that I was rewarded in this session with another piece of information. Indeed, this is how the future readings took shape by providing a piece of the jigsaw puzzle each time in the form of additional detail or information.

As time went on, it really did feel as if I was part of a large jigsaw and that it was my job to sort out all the pieces into some sort of order. It was a long, slow process and another test in patience!

5.

In the following October, I attended one of Tracey's self awareness courses in the hope that it would help me on my spiritual path and perhaps help to manifest the spiritual gift that I was purported to have. It seemed that Wulfgand was interested in the course too as he made himself known on several evenings including the first one when we each had to choose three coloured ribbons and then another member of the group had to do a reading from them. I chose two dark coloured ribbons and an orange one. Moira was drawn to read mine but did not like the feel of the two dark ribbons and felt it was something to do with death. At this point, Tracey intervened and explained that the two dark colours represented closely linked past lives with the female passing some years before the male. I felt that Wulfgand was in the background directing events in order to give me more evidence.

The next part of the course was equally intriguing and again gave the impression that events were being engineered by a higher force. After experimenting with psychometry, Tracey invited us to look through the various packs of tarot and oracle cards that she had in her collection. Tracey said that I might like to play with the runes and that my guide would like that as he is saying "Communication – at last". I picked three cards that I was drawn to which were really appropriate as they showed a partnership in the past, a period when I was standing still and a time when I am moving on. I was so impressed by the runes that Tracey let me borrow them for a week as she felt they were relevant for me. Over the following few days, I picked three runes. The first two both referred to a new life, a new path and a new beginning and focussed directly on self-change and an imminent connection with the divine. The third rune represented rebirth and said that work will be accomplished but the will must be clear and controlled. Blossoming will occur if modesty, patience, fairness and generosity are practised. Again, it seemed to me that I was being told of pending change and something new about to start. I wondered how much longer I would have to wait before I was aware of my spiritual gift or the work that I was meant to be doing. I then recalled the virtues mentioned on the third rune that I picked and realized that patience is the greatest virtue! However, I still felt that I was on the verge of something that I should be doing and so was determined to put those virtues into practice and to see if blossoming would occur.

6.

In November 2004, some friends of ours moved from Kent to a lovely Cornish cottage on the Lizard Peninsular, the most southerly point of Britain and they invited us to stay with them in the following February to celebrate their wedding anniversary and my husband's birthday which happened to fall on the same day. We were looking forward to this break especially when I looked at the map and realised that the Lizard was only about twenty-five miles from St. Ives. We now had a double incentive for making the trip to Cornwall that I had been longing to make for eleven years – a definite invitation to stay with friends and an opportunity to visit St. Ives and surrounding area where I lived with Wulfgand in our past life.

Tracey gave me another reading about this time and asked if I was going to Cornwall. Wulfgand was there with her and had a tear in his eye because I was going home. It was to be a spiritual journey for me and one where I would retrace my roots. Tracey could see me on my hands and knees kissing the earth on a grassy area on the edge of cliffs overlooking the sea. We lived on high ground so that we could see who approached.

I was excited by the thought of finding the village site but concerned that I would not be aware of the right place.

I knew it was in the area of St. Ives but that was all. Wulfgand told me not to worry because I would be led and that
I should go round the coast and ask for a feeling when it
was the right place. I must also clear my mind, ask him for
help and take a clear crystal which has been cleansed in salt
water. I felt it would be much easier if I could communicate
directly with Wulfgand but Tracey said as he is so close to
me, I will probably need a mediator but I will know when
he is around. It was reassuring to be told that Wulfgfand
was looking after me and that he will not let any harm come
to me.

It was at this session that the idea was introduced that
Eddie, my present husband, and I were somehow linked
previously and the link was in Cornwall. It was something
to do with the earth and pagan rites but at a different time.
Eddie is like a central stone with mediumistic people around
him and has been like that for a long time. This was intriguing and I wondered how it could possibly fit in with my
life with Wulfgand. However, no more information was
forthcoming so I had to be content with this complex piece
of the jigsaw and hoped I would be able to make it fit in
place one day.

As fate would have it, the trip to Cornwall had to be
postponed as my ninety-one year old mother had become
increasingly frail since Christmas and finally passed over
into spirit on 1st February 2005. It was a harrowing time
for all concerned and there was much sorting out to be
done during the following few months and so it was early
June before we made our way in a westerly direction. With
hindsight, this was advantageous as it gave me the chance
of two more readings which gave guidance from Wulfgand.
Without the extra detail given in these readings, I doubt
whether the search for the village site would have been as

successful as it was. This is just another example of events taking place when the time is right. I was not meant to go earlier – the time was not right and I did not have adequate information.

7.

The reading with Tracey in March 2005 was reassuring as Wulfgand said that he had taken good care of my mother just as I asked and that he knew we could not go to Cornwall because of her failing health leading to her death. However, he was waiting for me and said that something would lead me to the right place. I cannot move on until then although I have a spiritual job to do and he asked that I wear the necklace that belonged to mum when I go. This time, Wulfgand brought the children and said that I died in childbirth. He brought forward an old fashioned bowl of vegetable soup and asked if I had a cold. I have to admit that a cold was starting and developed fully two days later!

The final communication with Wulfgand before we left for Cornwall was at the end of May about a week before we were due to leave. Wulfgand had already told Tracey the previous night that I was going to find him and that he was excited that I was going home. He said that he will be with me and that I will know where he is. I must ask him to guide me and let me know when I am near. It is by the sea – a big grassy area overlooking cliffs and down to the sea and rocks. There is a white pub nearby but I have to go up to it and it is possible to drive some of the way. The place has a long name but the exact name was not forthcoming. I must wear my mother's necklace.

A scene now presented itself which was centred round my cremation and a burning body was shown on water. A young girl with long wavy hair was crying and standing by the riverbank while putting white flowers in the stream. It was my eldest daughter.

Soon after this poignant note, the session ended leaving me with a few more guidelines. I was beginning to feel the pressure building up as my friends' expectations were high. I just hoped and prayed that I would be receptive to Wulfgand's guidance and that I would find our village site.

8.

We arrived at our friends' beautiful Cornish cottage in the Lizard village on 5th June 2005. The sea was visible from our bedroom window and the stunning coastline of the Lizard Peninsular was only minutes away.

I was looking forward to our visit to St. Ives in a few days time and so, in preparation, I spent some time looking at a detailed Ordnance Survey map of the area. Each time I looked at the map, I was drawn to a coastal area just west of St. Ives town. I still needed to be more specific if I was to find the village site so I decided to use my crystal pendulum and asked Wulfgand for guidance. The pendulum pinpointed an area called Higher Burthallan and this is where I felt we should make for.

The day that we drove to St. Ives was warm and sunny and I was somewhat shocked at entering the town by a swarm of noisy holiday makers, a maze of tiny roads and one way systems with hardly room to navigate the hoards of people wandering around. It was forty years since my last visit and inevitably the town had grown but somehow I had expected it not to. All the car parks were full and we did a circuit of the town twice looking for somewhere to stop. I was beginning to wonder if we were ever going to be able to park when we spotted a space at the end of Porthmeor

Square, right outside a cottage door. It seemed a genuine parking space so we thankfully left the car there while we looked around. As I climbed out of the car, I looked up at the cottage and noticed that it was called "Norway Cottage". I felt that this was a good sign as I was wearing my mother's Norwegian necklace, as requested by Wulfgand. Being rather taken aback by so many people which destroyed any feelings that I was hoping to link into, we decided that the local museum would be a good place to start looking for clues which might lead us to the site of the village. The museum was only a short walk away and just as we entered the door a strange thing happened which obviously alarmed the staff judging by their reaction – all the lights went out for a few seconds and then came on again. To me, this was another relevant sign as Wulfgand had told me in an earlier communication that I would know when he was around as the lights would go up and down! I felt that we must be on the right track.

Although the museum was very interesting, nothing caught my attention and I felt very disappointed so I asked Wulfgand and the angels to guide me to Higher Burthallan. We went back to the car and discovered that we were indeed situated on the right road which led up to the area of Higher Burthallan. We drove up a narrow lane as far as we could go and then left the car on the verge at the entrance to a farm track. This seemed right to me and was in accordance with Wulfgand's earlier guidance when he said we had to go up but could drive up some of the way. We continued walking down the track until it turned into a footpath. By this time, the weather had turned and a thick sea mist covered the land. As we rounded a corner, I felt drawn to a field on the right and on the right of this field was a white house called "Fairway Farm". Was this Tracey's white pub which she said was nearby the site? I felt that it was. The field was a flattish area full of scattered boulders and large rocks and adjacent to a farm. I felt that this was the village site or at least, adjacent to it and my pendulum confirmed this. We continued walking along an overgrown footpath for about quarter of a mile until we reached a large grassy area with scattered rocks and boulders which sloped down to the cliff edge. Although the visibility was poor, I felt really excited and knew that there was a cove near and so ran to the right side of it and looked down from the clifftop to the steep ravine below. Just where I was standing, were beautiful large chrysanthemum type daisies and pink flowers as well as yellow irises and orchids further up by the little stream. In fact, there was a myriad of wild flowers everywhere – it was just so beautiful. I felt so excited that I ran further down the grassy area to the end where it overlooked the headland down to massive rocks and boulders and an odd shaped pool of water formed by high waves. At high tide, I guess the rocks would have formed a little island. It was a magical place to sit and listen to the waves crashing below. The visibility was now so poor as the sea mist closed in that most of the coastline was obliterated which was most disappointing but nevertheless I felt that this was the place where I had once lived and loved and my pendulum, again, confirmed it. On returning to the footpath, by which time a really bad headache had developed and the weather had turned much cooler, we passed the field entrance once more which looked quite ethereal in the mist and where there were now cows grazing between the boulders. I vowed to return as soon as possible and to choose a clear day in order to see the coastline in more detail.

My mind kept wandering back to the immense wealth of wild flowers there and how beautiful they were. Ten years ago, Wulfgand told me that I was always picking flowers during our life together – it is no wonder as I must have been surrounded by them and obviously appreciated them as much as I do today. The white daisies brought to mind the picture that Tracey had of my eldest daughter putting white flowers into the river where my cremation had taken place. Apart from the very small stream, no other waterway was obvious in the immediate vicinity and as the weather had deteriorated and time was running away from us, we were unable to explore further on this first visit. The whole place had a magical, mystical quality to it and I was certain that I had found my roots. I was now anxious to see if Wulfgand agreed!

Cliff edge near the village site - ethereal in sea mist

9.

As soon as it was possible, on our return from Cornwall, I went to see Tracey for a reading. Wulfgand was already there and confirmed that I had found the right place although he said that the village was a bit scattered and we were closer to the sea. Wulfgand was really pleased and had tears in his eyes because it was as if I was brought home. Although Wulfgand is very strong in character and form, he has a soft interior as shown by his emotion. Tracey asked if I had a headache while I was there at the site to which I replied that I had a very bad headache. This was a result of all the psychic messages trying to get through to me. Apparently, the chief of the village was pushing me out of the way as he was a bit annoyed that I was visiting because of the spiritual connection. The chief still guards the land and is very protective of the encampment and was somewhat miffed as I was linking in. However, he will get used to the idea I was told! Wulfgand was strong but the chief of the village was the strongest which demonstrated the fact that strength was all important in those days.

Tracey asked if there were daisies there as she could see me making a garland of white daisies to wear in my hair. White daisies are my spiritual sign I was told and of course, they were the first flowers that I noticed growing close to where I looked over the cliff into the cove. Incidentally, on returning home from Cornwall, the same white daisies were growing near the house in a small triangular border where I planted some nasturtiums and forget me nots with my small grandchildren during the previous year! It remains a mystery to me as to how they appeared there, unless of course, the spirit world had something to do with it. It seems too much of a coincidence to think otherwise.

Our village site was originally a place where people went for prayers when I first went there many centuries ago and at a later date it was also a place where witchcraft was practised. It is hardly surprising that the area had a mystical and mysterious air about it. There was also a big battle there in which Wulfgand was injured by a spearhead through the shoulder. Tracey felt sad that I did not find the river where my ashes were put as that is where my daughter is. The river is much smaller today than it was in our previous life I was told and is to the east of the village. My daughter was standing by the river carrying a young child and there was also a dead baby. She was saying goodbye to me. I promised to do my best to find the river during my next visit.

I wondered if my visit to Cornwall would act as a culmination of my partnership with Wulfgand and that maybe it would mark the end of our communication although I still felt that I was on the brink of something. However, Wulfgand had other ideas! I was told that the door was now open on my spiritual path and that I would be writing a book – a kind of love story which is our story. This is my quest in life and this is what I am meant to do. It will be inspired writing and Wulfgand will be helping me all the way. This idea had great appeal and, in fact, the idea had flashed through my mind once or twice but was instantly dismissed as I did not think spirit would approve. How wrong I was because now Wulfgand and others in the spirit world were clapping and were really happy with the idea. It was obvious that sessions with Wulfgand would continue and on a regular basis as he had more to tell.

This, then, was the point at which I started to research and write this book and Tracey's words of seventeen months ago came true when she said that I was unique and that I would understand when I started working. Writing is a solitary occupation mainly and unique insofar as no other people are around.

10.

Subsequent readings brought forth further details about our life together and our family. The pieces of the jigsaw were gradually being put together and an overall picture was beginning to emerge.

It seems that my love of dogs today has carried over from my previous life to my present one. Previously, a large dark coloured dog was part of our family. Apparently, he was always with me, followed me everywhere and used to lay down beside me while I was sitting by the outdoor fire making and repairing things. It was comforting to know that I had such a faithful guard dog whose presence was felt on several occasions.

I was about fifteen when we married and Wulfgand was a bit older. We had a good relationship and Wulfgand was very protective of me as he is today. The hut that we lived in was made of wooden planks from the top down to ground level so that it was quite dark inside. There was an earth floor covered with straw like material and we had a fire in the middle when the weather was cold in order to keep warm and to do the cooking. A wooden chest was hidden in the earth which contained our worldly goods, such as they were, and I wore the key to this all the time. Animal skins were used for bedding and although it sounds primitive by modern standards and no doubt strong smelling at times, it afforded protection from the elements and was possibly quite cosy in a basic sort of way.

Our family consisted of four daughters who led a happy life. They wore long gowns and often ran around in bare feet. One daughter had mousey coloured hair that she wore in plaits and another one had reddish hair, like her father. They looked a bit scruffy but were happy and enjoyed playing a game with stones on the floor of the hut. There was also an older girl who looked older than her years. One of them was born with a problem to do with her left arm and apparently most of their teeth were worn down! It seemed that not all survived and one child died of a fever despite being offered a herbal concoction of berries mixed in a bowl.

There was also an older boy who I brought up as my son although he was, in fact, Wulfgand's son by someone else even though there was no love between them. This son was born to Wulfgand when he was very young during his travels to England and he was born on a boat. His mother died on the journey and so he treated me like his mother and I was good to him. Wulfgand brought him forward now as he felt it was time to make him clear to me because I was unaware of his existence up to the present time. Wulfgand showed him as being about fifteen or sixteen with long hair, clean shaven and wearing a bandana round his head. He carried a long pointed stick or spear and went hunting with his father as well as helping him in the fields. It was a happy life but a hard existence.

11.

In 1993, when Wulfgand first made his appearance, he said that he was born in Germany and indicated that part which was known as Saxony. Many questions sprung to mind regarding his origins and his family and I hoped that some answers would be forthcoming in order for me to appreciate and understand his background. True to form, some answers came but the details were somewhat spasmodic and non specific and the jigsaw puzzle suddenly seemed almost too difficult to complete. A fascinating picture of Wulfgand's origins was building up but sadly, with many gaps in the details. I am the sort of person who likes to tie up any stray ends and to verify information as far as possible so hoped that further help and guidance would be given in the future.

From information gleaned so far, Wulfgand's family came originally from Norway and they travelled south in search of a better life. There were a lot of them and much fighting went on during their journey. They stopped at encampments on the way and there were mountains, rivers and lots of land all around. When travelling overland, they walked but also had wooden carts with no sides to them but with solid wheels. Wulfgand's mother was depicted as a pregnant lady who was riding on one of these carts and who was seen climbing down. A boy was born shortly afterwards and there were sisters.

Wulfgand was born in Germany on their travels and was born to fight he told me. On numerous occasions, he said that his people wrote the story about their travels on stone during their journey and showed a big boulder with runic inscriptions on it. It was situated near water but inland slightly and in the direction of the coast. The area was a bit hilly with a lot of tall trees around. A road sign was close by which sounded like "Gonnermaster". The family was travelling down towards the borders. Although Wulfgand was born in Germany, the family went back over the border in order to add his birth to the writing on the stone that had been started earlier. The stone still exists and was purportedly shown on a television programme about ten years ago.

I appreciate that spirit communication is not easy at the best of times but felt frustrated that no specific names or locations were forthcoming. The name "Gonnermaster" had no apparent meaning and obviously research was going to be time consuming and fraught with difficulties so I could only hope for further guidance. Nevertheless, the prospect was an exciting one and I was anxious to start the quest.

12.

Wulfgand said that he came to Britain when he was about fifteen and before the sea closed in. Before they left for England, Wulfgand and his people were forced to go inland, through the hills to the river and then out to sea in order to avoid some sort of tribe who did not want them on their land. The name "Nord" was heard which may be a clue to future research. A younger sister and his father accompanied Wulfgand but his mother had already died when he was quite young as a result of an accident when she was trapped by one of the carts after a battle. A lot of people took to boats and sailed down the river to the open sea and eventually landed in England. Their supplies included fruit that looked like apples and some sort of hard bread.

Wulfgand, with his family and friends, sailed to Cornwall as they considered it ideal land to conquer although it was inhabited by Celts at the time. On their arrival just west of St. Ives, they found an existing encampment which they took over by force. I was already living here at this encampment with an elderly blind man who was possibly a grandfather and whose eyes looked horrible as if they had been burnt or cut out. My mother was already dead and possibly a brother had died of a plague of some sort. My father was killed by Wulfgand's people when overtaking

the village and so it was not a good start to a relationship!
Despite this, when Wulfgand and I first met, it was love at
first sight although we had some difficulty understanding
each other's language.

13.

At this stage of the story, I turn my attention, once again to some research and this time into the Scandinavian peoples and their way of life in and around the eighth century to see if any light can be thrown onto Wulfgand's personal story and circumstances. I studied many articles and books on the Viking way of life and it was truly enlightening in an uncanny sort of way.

The first thing that was apparent was the fact that to a Viking, a ship was his home and a way of life. Sailing and rowing came as naturally as driving a car today and the rivers and fjords were their motorways. They were master ship builders and their long narrow boats that were flat bottomed had no need for harbours but were designed to be beached on any shelving shore. These boats could reach islets in shallow waters of estuaries that other boats could not navigate. Vikings were brave sailors and explorers who thought nothing of taking their families on long, dangerous journeys across the sea. As well as competent seafarers, the Norsemen were essentially farmers, fishermen and traders eking out their living from the land and the sea.

The term "Viking" has come to be applied to all Scandinavians of the period from the eighth to the beginning of the twelfth century but in the Viking age itself, the term

"Viking" applied only to someone who went "i viking", that is, plundering. In this sense, most Viking age Scandinavians were not Vikings at all but peaceful farmers and craftsmen who stayed quietly at home all their lives. For many others, being a Viking was just an occupation they resorted to for long enough to raise money to buy or acquire a farm and settle down.

The Scandinavian homeland was a remote region in a harsh environment. Norway, on the west of the Scandinavian peninsular is completely dominated by a long range of mountains known as "The Keel" in Viking times. The west coast is indented with deep fjords some of which penetrate over one hundred miles inland. Chains of islands and reef form a sheltered passage for shipping known as "The North Way" which gave Norway its name. The landscape has been scoured by ice and therefore the soil is generally thin, stoney, waterlogged and infertile except for Oslo and the Trondelag regions. The coast has cool summers and mild winters due to the Gulf Stream and its waters remain ice free in winter. Inland, the winters are severe with heavy snowfalls. The poverty of the soil was an incentive for seafaring as a supplement to hard living on the land. A shortage of good soils during the population growth may have led to land hunger and a reason for emigration in search of land to farm.

Most Scandinavians lived peacefully by agriculture, rearing animals and growing crops in small villages. In the marginal uplands of Norway and Sweden, hunting and fishing made a significant contribution to the diet as well as providing valuable trade goods. There are few large areas of fertile land in Norway and the broken nature of the terrain led to a dispersed settlement pattern with isolated farms on small pockets of cultivable land.

Scandinavian trade with the rest of Europe increased in the eighth century and probably encouraged the Viking expansion. It was mostly short distance and conducted by farmer/merchants from dozens of small ports round the coasts. This led to a small number of international trading places such as Hedeby, Ribe and Kaupang which developed into the first towns.

As well as the long, narrow boats, a deep sea trading ship called a "knarr" was used to carry settlers across the Atlantic to Iceland and Greenland in particular. These boats had wider, deeper and heavier hulls than the longships. Where convenient, they hugged the coast navigating by prominent landmarks ashore. The sun and stars were also used as navigational aids as well as orally transmitted practical knowledge of sea and weather conditions.

14.

During the late Germanic Iron Age of 600 – 800 AD, regional kingdoms or chiefdoms emerged such as Uppland in Sweden, Jutland in Denmark and Vestfold in Norway. Norway was divided up into roughly a dozen chiefdoms and petty kingdoms and local identities were strong. Not much is known about Sweden at this time but consisted of two main peoples – the Svear from around Lake Malaren and the Gotar from around Lake Vanern and Vattern. Denmark included modern Denmark, part of Germany and the provinces of Skane and Halland which are now in Sweden. There was also some sort of holding over Vestfold in Norway.

Denmark suffered an ongoing feud with the Franks from the lower Rhine over the border in Germany. The threat of Frankish expansion existed to the beginning of the Viking Age and was a reason that the Danevirke was built in 737 AD. This was an earthwork barrier built across the neck of the Jutland peninsular to protect Denmark from the south. It consisted of a series of fortifications from the River Treene to the head of Schleifjord and shielded the land route between the river Eider and Schleifjord. It was quite feasible, therefore, that Wulfgand's family had to travel inland to avoid the Frankish warriors who were protecting their land in Frisia.

At one stage, Wulfgand said that they left Europe before the sea came in. During my research, I came across the town of Dorestad which lay at the junction of the River Lek and an arm of the Rhine in the centre of the Netherlands. Dorestad was a huge trading centre in the eighth and ninth centuries but in 863 AD, the River Rhine changed its course and flooded the town. Could this be where Wulfgand and family set off from? It certainly fits in with his description of sailing down and out into the open sea which suggests a river and estuary.

Vikings voyaged far from their homes in Norway, Sweden and Denmark, driven by the lack of good farmland to seek new lands to settle and by the urge to plunder. Norwegians chiefly targeted Ireland, Scotland, Wales and Cornwall while the Danes headed for the north and east England and the Swedes headed east.

Saxons and Vikings were, in reality, very similar in their culture and traditions. They wore similar clothes – thick trousers and tunics for men, long dresses for women, leather shoes and woollen or fur cloaks in winter. They could understand each other's language, sharing also a common heritage of Germanic deities with traditional beliefs in spells and charms and the power of runic letters. Their songs and stories contained echoes of the same heroic deeds.

Their social and family structures were alike, as were there homes and farms. In battle, Saxon and Viking wielded similar weapons – swords, spears and axes. Most communities, like their Saxon counterparts, were made up of farmers living in small villages. A villager's home had a frame of wooden posts with wattle walls and a roof thatched with straw. It was crowded with three generations and animals commonly sharing the same house and smoky for the cooking fire burned in the middle of the dirt floor. Few houses had windows or much furniture apart from a wooden chest, beds, stools and perhaps a small table with clay pots and iron cauldrons for cooking and barrels for storage. The diet included bread, cheese, milk and eggs with beer brewed from barley and occasionally roast pork when the family pig was butchered.

Both Saxons and Vikings were skilled in carpentry and ironwork. Smiths forged practical items such as nails, door hinges and fish hooks from iron while the metalworkers fashioned exquisite brooches, pins, pendants and rings from materials including amber, jet, gold and silver. Saxons and Vikings shared a love of personal adornment with both men and women wearing jewellery. Wulfgand was gifted in carpentry skills and showed an intricately carved wooden toy that he made for the spirit children. It was a marvellous piece of skilled workmanship and this is what he enjoyed doing whenever he could.

Scandinavian smiths were highly skilled and warriors' weapons were richly decorated and proclaimed their status. Axes are the most often associated weapons of the Vikings and were a cheaper alternative to the sword which was the most favoured weapon. These were double edged longswords which were strong and flexible. Spears also had decorated blades. Bows and arrows and fighting knives were also used. The circular shield was a defensive weapon made of wood with iron bands to strengthen the rim and an iron boss to hold the grip. They were about three feet in diameter and protected the body from the neck to the thighs. These weapons were very similar to those used by Saxon warriors and as portrayed by Wulfgand himself at the very beginning of our communication.

The more I read about the history and times leading up to the mid eighth century, the more believable Wulfgand's revelations became. I always felt comfortable with him and sensed that he was a genuine character and I believed the story that was unravelling. However, when I began to unearth historical facts that fitted those that had already been told, I felt a sense of elation that the more sceptic minds among us might possibly begin to accept the idea of spirit communication. Indisputable evidence would of course, be in the existence of the stones that Wulfgand and family wrote on. Although the stones were said to still exist today, I have so little to go on and do not know for sure which country they are in. It would be a wonderful culmination of this book to locate them and I am determined to investigate as much as possible. Before doing so however, I felt that another trip to my Cornish roots was necessary before I could move on. A few loose ends needed to be tied up and some further research into the area needed to be carried out.

15.

An opportunity arose for my husband Eddie and me to take a short break away in Cornwall before the tourist season was in full swing. We stayed three nights in a country inn just outside St. Ives which was ideally placed for our needs.

One of the reasons for this visit was to look for the river where my cremation took place as I felt this was something I needed to do. Wulfgand had already said that he would guide me to the right place but that it is very different today and there may be only a trickle of water where once the river flowed. There was something about the coast that was different too. It was important to go to the site on Tuesday he said, so we decided to visit the Records Office in Truro on Wednesday which was the other reason for our visit as I wanted to research the area and to enquire if there were ever any witchcraft practices there. Wulfgand also showed me a green coloured book with gold on the edge and the title imprinted on the front and said to find out about witchcraft. I promised to remember this when carrying out enquiries.

Tuesday morning arrived bright and clear so we decided to make an early start. Tracey had already asked her Indian guide to help Wulfgand and me on this quest, so in preparation, I now dedicated my crystal pendulum and asked for guidance from both Wulfgand and Tracey's guide before

driving into St. Ives. We parked easily by Stennack School
and started to walk toward the town when I looked up and
saw the name "Norway House" on the side of a house high
above us. This was a good sign as I was wearing my mother's
Norwegian necklace again as on my first visit. This time I
wanted to approach the village site from the opposite direction along the cliff path so we set off for Porthmeor Beach
and the south west coastal path. The sun was shining and
the sea was a beautiful turquoise colour which contrasted
so well with the pale golden sands of the surf beach. The
visibility was crystal clear and the light was wonderful – no
wonder artists love it there. We set off on the coastal path
with the intention of finding the river where my ashes were.
We had only been walking a short while when the path
rounded a corner and in front of us was a black female figure baring her chest with painted face and wild hair! I was
slightly taken aback as it reminded me of witchcraft and
not what you would expect to find on a lonely coastal path.
It was, in fact, acting as a scarecrow (I presume) as it was
positioned next to some cabbages in a small plot of land. It
did make me wonder if any witchcraft was still practised in
this area today.

We passed two streams tumbling down from the higher
ground but continued walking until we reached Higher
Burthallan cliffs. The coastline was so clear and Godrevy
lighthouse and island were plain to see from the top – so different from our first visit when everything was shrouded in
mist. This is what I wanted to see and wondered if this was
the island that Tracey saw. Yellow gorse was in full bloom
all over the area as well as pale yellow primroses. There were
white horses at sea as it was quite breezy and the white surf
crashing against the rocks and the turquoise green sea was a
wonderful sight especially looking down into our deep cove
where the water was an amazing green. The high ground

had such an advantageous position as an approaching boat could be easily spotted from any direction. We left the coastal path and walked higher up towards the village site but were prevented from going further east in search of the river by dense scrubland. The path petered out and we were forced to return. Not knowing which way to go, I again called on Wulfgand and Tracey's guide to help and immediately found myself following a higher path than the one that we walked up on. My husband who was following, called out and said "I don't know where you're going but it might bring you out to where you want to be". We went up and up amongst the gorse until we came to a rocky outcrop with a fast running stream just before it. Although the stream was small, the whole area was wet and it was obvious that the water once covered a greater area. I felt sure this was where my ashes were and my crystal pendulum confirmed this. I stood listening to the trickling of the water running down the hillside with the constant sound of the sea in the background and felt a strange emotion wending its way up the left side of my body starting at my ankle and when it reached my head, the tears started to flow. The view from this spot was incredible – so utterly wild and natural but somehow familiar. I could almost see my daughter standing by the river and throwing a flower into the water – the feeling was very strong. In fact, there were yellow primroses, gorse and pink campion growing by the stream and I picked some of the flowers and put them in my press to include in the book as a gift for Wulfgand, as requested. I hope he is pleased with them. I also bottled some of the water from the stream to take home. While at home in Norfolk, I took a flint from my garden and put my energy into it. The flint was now laid in the stream thus returning my energy to this place.

*My promise to Wulfgand - flowers from
the area near our village*

At last, I had to tear myself away from this special spot so Eddie and I made our way down to the coastal path from whence we came. Keeping a watchful eye on the outcrop and the course of the river down the hillside, we worked out which of the two streams that we passed was "my" stream – again with the help of my pendulum. The water babbled down the hillside, went under the coastal path and came out the other side and then cascaded over the cliff down to the sea. I felt my mission had been completed.

Next, I felt drawn to visit the village of Lelant which is just outside St. Ives and backs onto the Hayle estuary. I believe this is where Wulfgand landed his boat on first arriving from overseas before looking for a suitable encampment. Although the tide was out, the Hayle Bar was obvious and the river in full flow. It was easy to imagine a long boat sailing round the coast and into the sheltered waters of the estuary. The three miles of golden sandy beaches stretched away in the distance and I wondered if the coast here looked the same when Wulfgand arrived.

An amazing day ended by watching an incredible sunset over the sea and Higher Burthallan cliffs. The sky and the clouds turned to such wonderful colours and the striped pattern and glow of the clouds resembled the aurora borealis. The cliffs of Burthallan looked as if they were surrounded by a golden aura. It was a wonderful sight and one that I will remember for a long time to come.

16.

The following day was set aside for a visit to the Records Office in Truro to see if there were any historical maps or data that might be of interest. Although we had not booked an appointment as we were on a flying visit, so to speak, we spoke to a very helpful lady who gave us several leads and advice and who showed us an index of place names in which Burthallan was included. It used to be called Bosworthallan and she told us that the prefix "bos" precedes "tre" meaning "dwelling" and so indicates an early settlement. This was encouraging and I felt that I could mention to her the fact that I was interested in finding out if any witchcraft practices were carried out in the area. Almost immediately she said that it was quite probable as that particular area and West Penwith in general was riddled with folklore and witchcraft practices more than anywhere else. They are called "pellars" in Cornwall and she gave me information and directions to the Cornwall Centre in Redruth which is the home of the Cornish Studies Library and which has Cornwall's largest collection of printed and published books and pamphlets about Cornwall as well as the largest collection of journals, magazines, newspapers, photographs, parish registers and so on.

The knowledge that witchcraft was practised along that coast fitted in with the theory that Eddie was once a white witch or should I say pellar and was hanged for his beliefs. I began to feel that questions were being answered and evidence uncovered and that the pieces of the jigsaw were fitting into place. A visit to Redruth was a must to see if any information on pellars could be unearthed.

It was now suggested that we call into the Historic Environment Service which was part of the same County Hall complex to see if anyone could locate a map of the area. By now, it was lunchtime and again, not having booked an appointment, we did not hold out much hope but decided to call on the offchance. A very friendly and helpful member of staff (whose lunch must have been interrupted and I apologise for that) brought up various maps of Higher Burthallan and area on screen including the large scale nineteenth century Ordnance Survey map which showed the field numbers and other landmarks. The archaeological map was also brought up which was very interesting as it showed medieval field systems and in the experience of the archaeologists, this generally meant that they were on sites of earlier settlements. I felt quite excited by this discovery as, at last, I had some concrete evidence that a settlement of some kind did actually exist on what I felt was my village site. This particular map also showed the remains of two medieval buildings or of later date described as "picts houses" which were stone built huts of an irregular shape. This excited me even more to think that there were dwellings here in medieval times or a later date which tied in with the theory that Eddie, my husband, also lived in this same area but centuries later than me. Furthermore, these two buildings were positioned on the land a bit closer to the sea than my village site and where I previously felt that Eddie's withcraft practices were carried out. This was corroboration indeed and we left the office armed with copies of maps and aerial photographs and feeling very pleased with our discoveries.

On our way home the next day, we called into the Cornwall Centre where I explained to a young lady that I was interested in any evidence of witchcraft in the St. Ives area. Apparently, the staff all specialize in a different subject and withchcraft was this young lady's special subject. I was obviously meant to be there at that particular time and she told me that the area from St. Ives to Zennor (and Burthallan is somewhere in the middle) is riddled with stories of pellars and witchcraft. There is even a Witches Rock and a Wicca Cove still marked on the map today.

We were directed to the section of books on witchcraft and the assistant pointed out several volumes that she thought might be helpful and that would explain more about the pellars. Three of these books were green in colour with gold writing on the edge and front and I immediately remembered that Wulfgand had brought forward such a book at our last session. These three volumes were written by William Bottrell in the 1870's and are about tradition and folklore in Cornwall. There was a section describing a pellar as being someone, mostly male, who practised white witchcraft in the sense that he was a herbalist and healer, a fortune teller and a conjuror. A pellar was one of the cunning folk who was an occult practitioner and an inheritor of the native witchcraft tradition from the seventeenth century. The practice of witchcraft was widespread and consisted of a set of beliefs and practices that were rooted in tradition. The Cornish believed in the power of herbal remedies that were gathered for drying at full moon.

During the mid 1600's, legislation (The Witchcraft Act) under King James led to the widespread condemnation of the old craft and during the seventeenth century many were brought to trial as it was the heyday of persecutions. It would appear that the inquisition of this period verged on the paranoia and propaganda was rife that those accused were black witches who caused harm to others when in fact, the opposite was true. The pellars were the most powerful of all witches and their reputation survived into the late nineteenth century. Spring was the time when most people visited the pellar in order to renew protection for their crops and animals for the coming year and to ward off evil influences. Pellars would also be called on to remove curses and ill luck.

Early records of trials and accusations have not survived unfortunately and there appears to be little written evidence of persecutions in the St. Ives area. However, from the information gleaned, it would appear to be quite feasible that my husband was hanged for carrying out his traditional craft of a pellar in his former life. Strangely enough, Eddie has always been interested in health and medicine and would have pursued the career of a doctor if circumstances had been different. As it is, he is drawn to complimentary medicine today and will often disappear into the herb garden to concoct a remedy for a sore throat or an upset stomach. His knowledge of acupressure points for aches and pains is renowned among family and friends who have benefited. It seems that his traditional beliefs have been brought forward to this incarnation. Moreover, he is totally against wearing a tie. Hidden memories of a noose perhaps!

17.

The communication with Wulfgand on returning home to Norfolk, confirmed that I had indeed located the right stream but it is much smaller today, he said. They were all standing by me at the stream and my daughter who was standing on my left, put her hand on my shoulder. This must have been the cause of the strong emotion that I felt working its way up the left side of my body. Wulfgand was really happy that I went home again and said that the cliffs looked a bit different in days gone by as there was some sort of a castle on the rocks. This tied in with something I read in one of the books I referred to in Cornwall which said that there used to be many fortified places along the coast at West Penwith known as cliff castles. It was also confirmed that Lelant was the place where he landed his boat on first arriving in Cornwall although it was slightly more towards the headland from where I was.

A few weeks later, another character made an appearance whose purpose was to try to explain in more detail, Eddie's time in Cornwall and the link connecting us. The name of this bearded character was Sampson or Samuel and he wore a cloak with black trousers to the knee and a hat under the cloak hood. The year 1784 was categorically told to us. This person was very gifted and well liked and people looked up to him as being a very magical and powerful person. He knew about plants and was a very wise man. Tracey was now shown a lot of people gathered round a fire who were carrying out some sort of ritual to do with the sun. There was a large tree part of which formed a table top on which was placed a lock of hair, some beads and something wrapped in brown cloth. The moon was shining and there were lanterns burning so that the scene appeared in an eerie light and the sea was visible in the background. Tracy now heard people approaching on horseback and women started to scream and others were climbing down the cliff to the cove to escape. It appeared to be some sort of raid in which Sampson/Samuel was grabbed from behind and stabbed in his left shoulder and was later hung on the spot without a trial. He was fifty-five years old. This man was Eddie and the last hours of his former life were being played out. An older lady who was a friend and who helped him after his wife died, showed a stone house nearby where he lived. On the night that he died, Sampson/Samuel was casting a spell on the land to reunite souls, including his love and as I died in that same place, albeit centuries apart, he brought my spirit forward, thus we were connected. Before he could finish, he was attacked and arrested but our spirits had already been brought together. In order to complete the cycle, our souls had to come back to earth. It took some time to find each other in this life but now that we have, he feels his life is fulfilled. We were both spiritually powerful people in our former lives and have a special bond now.

This certainly helped to clarify the link and the events surrounding it were lucidly depicted. The stone house nearby that was shown was possibly one of the two stone huts shown on the archaeological map of the area. It would seem that Eddie did indeed live in the area where I felt he carried out his witchcraft practices.

If only I could find out if the houses were inhabited in 1784, who lived in them and if anyone died in that year, in that area called Samuel or Sampson. It was a long shot but one I felt had to be pursued as far as possible.

18.

The most logical next step, of course, was another visit to the Cornwall Record Office in Truro to make a search of the relevant burial register but that involved a round trip of nearly six hundred miles and time away from home which was not possible at this particular time. The next best thing was the internet which has been a godsend for many family historians and researchers alike.

After locating the appropriate records and catalogue numbers, I posted off a request for a copy of the burial entries for the years 1780 –1790 at St. Ives. Several weeks elapsed and I was beginning to feel that my patience was being tested again! This written story is certainly not meant to be rushed as the pieces of the puzzle are only revealed a little at a time. At last, after a month, an envelope arrived in the postbox with the Cornish Record Office stamp on it. With bated breath, I tore the envelope open to find extremely faint copies of the burial entries. Some pages were worse than others according to the condition of the originals but they were just about legible. I read through the entries for 1784 but was disappointed that there was no-one by the name of Samuel or Sampson. However, the fist entry in early January of 1785 was a Samuel Bennet. I felt quite excited by this find but as there were no details of the cause of death or even his age, I could not be sure that this was my man.

On further perusal, I found an Elizabeth Bennet who died a few years earlier in 1779. Was this Samuel's wife? It seemed to fit as I knew that the pellar named Sampson or Samuel had a wife who had died previously and who he was trying to link with on the night of the raid. However, I felt I needed to dig a bit deeper so it was back to the computer where I searched through hundreds of names and although there were no marriages of a Samuel Bennet and an Elizabeth in St. Ives, I found just such a marriage in another parish. Furthermore, I found a birth of a Samuel Bennett in the same parish in 1727 which would make him fifty-seven in 1784 and not fifty-five as we were told but two years is neither here nor there as any family researcher will tell you. I felt that this Samuel could most probably be the one whose marriage I found and who died in St. Ives in 1785. I then noticed the name of his father and almost jumped out of my skin as the name of Sampson Bennett leapt out at me. I have never come across a christian name of Sampson before and when Tracey was told this name, I immediately thought it was a surname. These revelations seemed too much of a coincidence as they fitted in with the information given by spirit.

The earliest map of the area of Burthallan cliff that was available was dated 1824 and did not show any buildings where the remains of the stone huts were so that was disappointing. After further research into manorial records, it was discovered that a John Bennett, a James Bennett and a Robert Bennett all leased land in the Burthallan area during the 1850's and before. This was interesting as it proved that a family by the name of Bennett lived in the area albeit sixty years later. Were they related to Samuel Bennett and did he also live in this area a generation or two earlier? It would seem very likely on the strength of the evidence that has unfolded but I will leave the reader to decide for himself. Maybe, at a later date, when time allows, I will dig a little deeper in order to unearth further proof but for the time being, this will suffice. I feel that the results of my research are well founded.

19.

The only remaining piece of the jigsaw to investigate was the question of the runestones that Wulfgand's people wrote on during their travels. I therefore decided to do some general research into runestones to see if the information given was feasible.

I learnt that all barbarian tribes such as Goths, Franks, Saxons, Jutes and Scandinavians spoke Germanic languages. Some had their own mode of writing using a distinctive runic alphabet, each letter of which was called a rune. Earliest extant runes are dated to the second century and the script continued in use in some regions throughout the Middle Ages and into early modern times.

Runic script was designed for inscribing, at first on wood, then metal, bone and stone. Runes were not designed for writing in our sense of the word but to convey simple, short messages.

The traveller through Sweden will often have observed standing stones with inscriptions on them in a runic script, set up by waysides, at river crossings or on open greens. These are the famous runestones which are found to a lesser degree all over Scandinavia and even some inscribed artefacts have been found in north western Europe and the Low

Countries. Some texts read from left to right and some from right to left.

During the fifth to seventh centuries, runes were in common use in central Germany but disappear with the coming of Christianity. Evidence suggests the runic script spread from the heartland in the north to the south and east. This is partly due to the movement of peoples who travelled through Europe but also to cultural contacts between different Germanic peoples.

The earliest runestones seem to be Norwegian followed by those in Sweden and by the early eighth century , they appeared in Denmark. They are the first examples of memorial type providing evidence of language, history, political events and social conditions but some had single names on the gravestone or memorial stone. Runic inscriptions contributed to our knowledge of Norse history as they reflect the views and actions of the time. Great runestones were so characteristic of the age (700 – 1100AD) and were often memorials commemorating those who died far from home or the great who had died. Some Vikings put up stones in their own honour to boast of deeds that they thought praiseworthy. Most were free standing and were often natural boulders. Occasionally, a runemaster would cut an inscription on the face of a living rock that could be seen at a distance or by a road or river crossing. Some have decorative carvings and some would be coloured in although little remains of paintwork today. The most famous of all runestones is the Jelling Stone in the town of Jylland, Denmark and commemorates the royal family and a major burial.

Runestones would also act as a newspaper today by publishing a man's death in a public place such as at a meeting field or by a main roadside and so on. They may record the circumstances of death, place of burial, major events in his life, relationship to the living etc. Some stones record

Viking enterprise in the west and adventures abroad while some show inheritance and family ties which give important genealogical information.

In the light of this information, it would indeed seem highly probable that Wulfgand's family did write of their travels on natural boulders for all to see. Maybe they have survived the centuries and are still standing. Maybe they are covered in moss and the inscriptions are illegible or maybe they are still standing and are plain to see. Although it was my greatest hope to locate them in order to give positive proof from spirit, I realize that at the present time, it is inconceivable and beyond the scope of this story. I realize that the lack of precise locations would make it an impossible task and cannot be included in this book but in the future, I will continue to investigate the few clues that have been given so far as and when I feel the time is right. Who knows, a few more clues may come my way to help in my search. I sincerely hope so.

20.

As mentioned earlier, I died giving birth to our fifth child when I was not yet thirty years of age and before I could say goodbye properly to the family. After I died, my eldest daughter looked after the younger ones, helped by my own sister. This must have been extremely hard for her and she was seen standing by the river carrying a younger child and she was saying goodbye to me. There was also a very young baby who had died and this must have been my fifth daughter who died a few weeks after birth. This river, which contains my ashes, is patently an important and poignant place in my history and I feel privileged to have been guided to its whereabouts during my visit to the area.

View towards St. Ives from the river

Wulfgand was killed in battle in 763 AD, not long after my death but he did not care as life without me was not the same. This was the ending of our previous life together but as you die, you live and the ending is but a beginning. Our story has come full circle and our souls have been reunited proving that love does stand the test of time. The concluding part of the story will be, of course, when my spirit once again joins Wulfgand in the next world but I hope that will not be for some time to come as I have other work to complete here on earth!

Here, I am fulfilling my earthly life with my husband Eddie who is the third side of the spiritual triangle and who, of course, was the Cornish pellar who died whilst linking with my spirit. We are now completing our life together and it is proving to be a rewarding experience. When the time comes, we look forward to meeting Wulfgand in the spirit world thus reuniting all three souls and within the full circle, we will all be one.

Epilogue

Since the completion of this story, something has come to light that was mentioned and left unexplained in Part 1 and this is the significance of the multi pointed star that was drawn during the initial writings. Wulfgand now tells me that it is to do with Eddie and the link between us. It is certainly very reminiscent of the pentacle or five pointed star which is the Celtic symbol of earth and which I had already decided to use to decorate the book cover. The earth or land was the link between Eddie and myself in Cornwall so the explanation was staring me in the face but I could not see it! This link was only made known during the last twelve months, so when the star was drawn twelve years ago, Wulfgand was right when he said that it was a symbol of old and that I would recognise it.

Incidentally, as the county of Yorkshire is dear to Eddie's heart, the symbol of the white rose of York was engraved on bracelets that we exchanged on our marriage in 1998. The outer petals and leaves on this emblem form five points and look suspiciously like the pentacle!

About the Author

I was born in 1946 and brought up in Surrey where I lived until I was twenty. My childhood was a happy and carefree one and I particularly loved the primary school "on the green" where my father had also gone to school a generation before. Grammar school followed and then teachers' training college (which I did not pursue). I married in 1972 and my love of the countryside took us to rural Norfolk where I worked as a local government officer for thirty years.

My second marriage took place in 1998 and many happy years were spent riding our motorbikes both at home and abroad. We moved into the converted barns that my husband owned with half an acre of garden where we have lived for the last ten years. Since taking early retirement, I sold my motorbike and decided to concentrate more on my spiritual interests and now practise Reiki healing, Indian Head Massage and yoga as well as having a keen interest in genealogy, gardening, beekeeping and playing the piano. I have three step children and five grandchildren who live in different parts of the country who love to visit when they can. The children especially love Henny, my one surviving chicken who has been part of the establishment for seven years and is quite a personality!

During the last ten years, we have enjoyed travelling and realized personal dreams by visiting many faraway places including Nepal, India and New Zealand as well as destinations closer to home.

My family and friends consider me to be level headed and down to earth and I hope that this aspect of my character will be apparent in my writing and recording of details on a subject which some might consider to be the result of an overactive imagination.

Printed in the United States
112226LV00002B/11/A

9 781434 300447